D1708908

BALTIMORE

ORIOLES

BY STEPH GIEDD

SportsZone

An Imprint of Abdo Publishing
abdobooks.com

abdobooks.com

Published by Abdo Publishing, a division of ABDO, PO Box 398166, Minneapolis, Minnesota 55439. Copyright © 2023 by Abdo Consulting Group, Inc. International copyrights reserved in all countries. No part of this book may be reproduced in any form without written permission from the publisher. SportsZone™ is a trademark and logo of Abdo Publishing.

Printed in the United States of America, North Mankato, Minnesota.
102022
012023

Cover Photo: Joe Robbins/Icon Sportswire/AP Images
Interior Photos: Brian Bahr/AFP/Getty Images, 4; Mitchell Layton/Getty Images Sport/ Getty Images, 7, 39, 40; Bettmann/Getty Images, 9, 19; AP Images, 10, 12; Diamond Images/Getty Images, 14; Focus on Sport/Getty Images, 16, 20, 27, 29, 33; Focus on Sport/Getty Images Sport/Getty Images, 18, 22; Jerry Wachter/Sports Imagery/Getty Images Sport/Getty Images, 24; Ron Vesely/MLB Photos/Getty Images Sport/Getty Images, 26; John Reid III/MLB Photos/Getty Images Sport/Getty Images, 30; Nick Wass/AP Images, 34; Ben Margot/AP Images, 37

Editor: Charlie Beattie
Series Designer: Becky Daum

Library of Congress Control Number: 2022940389

Publisher's Cataloging-in-Publication Data

Names: Giedd, Steph, author.
Title: Baltimore Orioles / by Steph Giedd
Description: Minneapolis, Minnesota: Abdo Publishing, 2023 | Series: Inside MLB | Includes online resources and index.
Identifiers: ISBN 9781098290108 (lib. bdg.) | ISBN 9781098275303 (ebook)
Subjects: LCSH: Baltimore Orioles (Baseball team)--Juvenile literature. | Baseball teams--Juvenile literature. | Professional sports--Juvenile literature. | Sports franchises--Juvenile literature. | Major League Baseball (Organization)--Juvenile literature.
Classification: DDC 796.35764--dc23

TABLE OF

CONTENTS

LONG JOURNEY HOME

Cal Ripken Jr. stepped out of the dugout at Oriole Park at Camden Yards on September 6, 1995. His Baltimore Orioles were preparing to host the California Angels. But first, a crowd of 46,272 fans, all celebrating him, let out a roar.

An old railroad warehouse sits across a plaza behind right field at the stadium. On its wall hung a banner that read "2,130."

That marked how many consecutive games Ripken had played without a single day off, making his mark as the current "iron man" of Major League Baseball (MLB). Once the game became official, he would break the record held for 62 years by former New York Yankees star Lou Gehrig.

Cal Ripken Jr. salutes the Baltimore crowd during his record-breaking game on September 6, 1995.

The score was tied 1–1 going into the bottom of the fourth inning. Facing a 3–0 count, Ripken got a fastball right down the middle. He knew this was the pitch to make his mark on an already historic game. The ball ripped off his bat down the left-field line. It was over the wall in a flash for a home run. The crowd stood and cheered. No one sat down even after the shortstop returned to the dugout. As the fans continued to show their appreciation, Ripken returned to the field and tipped his hat.

PRESIDENTIAL CALL

President Bill Clinton was on the air in the broadcast booth at Camden Yards on the night that Ripken broke Lou Gehrig's consecutive game record. When the count got to 3–0, Clinton told legendary broadcaster Jon Miller that Ripken would be swinging at anything over the plate. After Ripken's blast cleared the fence, both the president and Miller stood and joined the fans' ovation.

The moment everyone was truly waiting for came soon after. Once the top half of the fifth inning passed, the game became official. Even if it had to be cut short due to weather or some other reason, the game would count in the standings. That meant Ripken had his record. The game halted to celebrate the feat. The "0" on the banner in right field fell, revealing a "1."

In a show of gratitude to the fans, Ripken took the time to jog around the entire stadium.

The legendary shortstop high-fived as many fans as he could. Along the way around the park, he soaked in the cheers from the Orioles' adoring fans.

"The celebration of 50,000 started to be very one-on-one and very personal. I started seeing people I knew," Ripken said. "Those were the people that had been around the ballpark all those years, and it was really a wonderful human experience."

Ripken watches his fourth-inning home run leave Oriole Park at Camden Yards.

FROM BREWERS TO BROWNS

More than 90 years before Ripken set his record, his hometown Orioles got their start. But the team was far away from Baltimore. The Orioles began as the Milwaukee Brewers in 1901. They were one of the first teams in the newly formed American League (AL).

The team didn't stay in Milwaukee for long. After a 48–89 season, the Brewers were off to St. Louis. There they changed their name to the Browns. A new city didn't bring better results. Despite featuring stars such as future Hall-of-Fame shortstop Bobby Wallace, the Browns struggled. In their first 20 seasons, they finished higher than fourth place only twice.

A breakthrough finally came in 1922. The Browns now had one of the game's best hitters. First baseman George Sisler batted .420 that year, the second-highest average in AL history. That hitting prowess earned Sisler the AL Most Valuable Player (MVP) Award. Behind Sisler and slugging outfielder Ken Williams, the Browns remained in the race all year. Meanwhile, ace Urban Shocker added 24 wins and an AL-best 149 strikeouts. However, the Browns came up just short. They finished one game back of the champion New York Yankees. With no playoffs at the time, the Yankees went on to the World Series while the Browns went home.

Shocker was traded to the Yankees after the 1924 season. Sisler and Williams each lasted a few more years in St. Louis. But the Browns never rose so high again in the 1920s or 1930s.

ST. LOUIS SERIES

For much of the Browns' history, they competed for fans with the St. Louis Cardinals of the National League (NL). The teams shared Sportsman's Park. However, the Cardinals captured most of the city's attention. That was especially true after they became a powerhouse in the 1930s. The Browns struggled to keep up.

In 1941 the United States entered World War II (1939–45). Many young men signed up to fight, including baseball players. With many of the biggest MLB stars overseas, baseball saw

George Sisler's 257 base hits during the 1920 season set an MLB record that stood until 2004.

many unusual events in the early 1940s. One of them was a rare good season for the Browns.

In 1944 the Browns improved to 89–65. That was good enough to win the AL. The Cardinals won the NL. For the first time since 1923, when the Yankees defeated the New York Giants, two teams from the same city met in the World Series. After taking a 2–1 series lead, the Browns scored only two runs in the final three games and lost 4–2.

US senator from Missouri and future president Harry Truman, *center*, poses with Browns' manager Luke Sewell, *left*, and Cardinals' manager Billy Southworth before Game 3 of the 1944 World Series.

As stars returned from the war, the Browns dropped in the standings. By 1947 they were once again in last place.

BILL'S BIG SHOW

In 1950 the Browns drew fewer than 250,000 fans, last in the AL. The next year the team had a new owner. Bill Veeck Jr. was known for having one of the most creative minds in baseball. He tried everything to draw fans and save the team's future in St. Louis.

During the 1951 season, Veeck signed 3-foot-7-inch Eddie Gaedel. Veeck's idea was that with the shorter player's small strike zone, he could draw walks easily. Gaedel came to bat only once, on August 29, against the Detroit Tigers. His uniform number read "1/8." Sure enough, Detroit Tigers' starter Bob Cain walked Gaedel on four pitches. After the plate appearance, Gaedel was immediately removed for a pinch runner. When the contest was over, AL president William Harridge called Gaedel's signing a "mockery of the game." Harridge quickly canceled Gaedel's contract. A week later, Veeck staged "Grandstand Managers Night." Fans voted on what the Browns should do next by holding up signs that read "yes" on one side and "no" on the other.

Other owners hated Veeck's stunts. Fans in St. Louis loved them and started showing up to the park. But even so, Veeck was still losing money. In 1953 he decided to sell the Browns to a group of businessmen from Baltimore. The next year, the team was on the move again.

A FAMILY BUSINESS

There have been three generations of Veecks in the baseball world. Bill Veeck Sr. was the president of the Chicago Cubs from 1919 to 1933. Following in his footsteps was Bill Jr., who owned three different MLB teams in his career. Bill Jr.'s son Mike is involved in the ownership of several minor league teams.

CHAPTER 2

BUILDING A WINNER

After 52 years in St. Louis, the Browns were off to Maryland. Today's Baltimore Orioles began play in 1954. Multiple previous baseball teams in Baltimore had been named the Orioles. Following the Browns' move, they decided to take on this nickname as well.

In 1954 Paul Richards became the Orioles' general manager. A year later he took over managing on the field. Meanwhile, Jim McLaughlin ran the team's farm system. Together, they developed a team philosophy to scout, sign, and teach players. Every coach in the Orioles' system followed the pair's direction, so players were taught the same ideas all the way up to the majors.

Manager Jimmy Dykes waves to the crowd welcoming the Orioles to Baltimore with a parade in 1954.

The Oriole Way helped develop Baltimore's future stars like third baseman Brooks Robinson.

Richards and McLaughlin stressed fundamental baseball. Richards liked to say, "The simple things in baseball number into the thousands." If Orioles players could master all the little skills, the team would be successful. The system became known as "the Oriole Way."

It took six years, but by 1960, Baltimore began to see results. The Orioles stayed in contention until the final two weeks of the season. That gave McLaughlin and Richards proof that the Oriole Way was working.

Richards left the Orioles a year later to take over the Houston Astros in his home state of Texas. But his teachings stayed behind in Baltimore. And the Orioles were on the path to victory.

BIRDS TAKE FLIGHT

By 1966 the Orioles had an exciting team. Two young pitchers, Dave McNally and Jim Palmer, led a strong staff. First baseman Boog Powell and outfielder Paul Blair were both budding stars. Third baseman Brooks Robinson was the 1964 AL MVP, and he was on his way to the seventh of 16 Gold Glove Awards. And before the 1966 season began, the Orioles made one of baseball's most lopsided trades ever. The team sent three players to the Cincinnati Reds for former NL MVP Frank Robinson. He led the league with 49 home runs, 122 runs batted in (RBIs), and a .316 batting average. Frank Robinson's Triple Crown season made him the first person to earn MVP in both the AL and the NL. The move put the Orioles over the top.

PREVIOUS BIRDS

Long before the current Orioles, three previous teams played in Baltimore using that nickname. The original Orioles played in the NL and the American Association from 1882 to 1899. They then spent two years in the AL before folding. Two different minor league teams called the Orioles existed from 1903 to 1953. Legendary slugger Babe Ruth, a Baltimore native, played his minor league ball for the Orioles before the Boston Red Sox purchased his contract in 1913.

In the World Series, the upstart Orioles met the powerhouse Los Angeles Dodgers. The NL champions had won the World

Frank Robinson's Triple Crown season of 1966 was the only time he ever topped his league in batting average, home runs, or RBIs.

Series in 1963 and 1965 behind the dominant pitching duo of righty Don Drysdale and lefty Sandy Koufax. But Baltimore's young rotation was also strong. Palmer, a future Hall of Famer, won 15 games. McNally won 13, and Wally Bunker added 10. All three starters were 23 years old or younger.

Frank Robinson set the tone early in Game 1. The slugger got the Orioles going with a two-run homer in the first inning off Drysdale. Brooks Robinson followed up with a solo shot in the next at-bat. McNally struggled through 2 1/3 innings. But reliever Moe Drabowsky came in and shut down Los Angeles. He finished the game, striking out 11 batters to get the 5–2 win.

PUTTING UP ZEROES

Game 2 saw a matchup of Palmer and Koufax. The Dodgers' lefty was considered the era's best pitcher. He completed 27 of his 41 starts in 1966. However, the Orioles knocked Koufax out after six innings. The 20-year-old Palmer, meanwhile, became the youngest pitcher ever to throw a World Series shutout, striking out six. The Orioles won 6–0 in what turned out to be Koufax's last game. He retired after the series at age 30 due to an injured elbow.

When Game 3 started, the Dodgers had not scored in 15 1/3 innings. In the first World Series game ever held in Baltimore,

Jim Palmer allowed only four hits during his Game 2 shutout of the Los Angeles Dodgers in the 1966 World Series.

Bunker kept the shutout streak going with another complete game. Blair provided all the offense the Orioles needed with a 430-foot home run in the fifth inning. The 1–0 victory pushed Baltimore to the brink of a title.

McNally and Drysdale both returned for Game 4. This time, each pitcher dominated. But it was Frank Robinson who broke the deadlock again. With one out in the fourth, he crushed Drysdale's first pitch to left field for the 1–0 lead.

The home-run pitch was Drysdale's only mistake. The problem for the Dodgers came from McNally, who had allowed only three hits through seven innings. He received defensive help in the eighth. Blair hadn't started the game, but manager Hank Bauer put him in center field for defense before the inning started. Blair made his manager look like a genius. Los Angeles's leadoff hitter Jim Lefebvre hit McNally's 3–2 pitch

Dave McNally, *right*, celebrates the final out of the 1966 World Series with third baseman Brooks Robinson.

deep to center. Blair leaped up and pulled the potential tying home run back over the fence for an out.

McNally put two runners on with one out in the ninth. But a lineout and a fly-out ended the game. The Orioles had pitched an incredible three shutouts in a row. And for the first time ever, Baltimore celebrated a World Series champion.

A WINNING REPUTATION

Baltimore stumbled to a losing record in 1967. However, the Orioles didn't stay down for long. After a slow start to the next season, Earl Weaver replaced Hank Bauer as manager. Weaver went 48–34 in 1968 as the Orioles won 91 games. It wasn't good enough to reach the World Series that year. But it was a sign that Baltimore was ready to take over the AL again.

The short, stocky Weaver proved to be a managing genius. When it came to his players, Weaver was calm and collected. But with the umpires, he could get a little heated. He was constantly arguing and frequently ejected from games. No matter the method, Weaver was effective. In an era when

Earl Weaver's 1,480 victories with the Orioles are more than 800 higher than the team's second-winningest manager.

Offensive stars like Baltimore's Boog Powell, *right*, were frustrated by the Mets' talented pitching staff during the 1969 World Series.

managers looked for bunts and stolen bases, Weaver didn't want either. He wanted his offense to put up big innings.

Of course, Weaver knew that his standout pitching staff would back up the runs his team scored. In 1969 Weaver's starters included Jim Palmer, Dave McNally, and 32-year-old lefty Mike Cuellar. He won 23 games and the AL Cy Young Award, given to the top pitcher in the league. With Boog Powell, Paul Blair, Brooks Robinson, and Frank Robinson still slugging, the Orioles looked unbeatable.

That was certainly what everyone thought as Baltimore cruised to 109 wins. That season saw the introduction of the AL Championship Series (ALCS). Baltimore made short work of the Minnesota Twins in a three-game sweep.

The World Series looked like one of the all-time mismatches. Opposing the Orioles were the New York Mets. The Mets had been founded in 1962. And until 1969, they had been awful. However, the team turned it around and finished 100–62.

Despite the close records, it shocked baseball when the Mets scored the upset. Baltimore won the first game, then lost four straight. Mets pitchers Jerry Koosman and Tom Seaver shut Baltimore's offense down. And they were backed by several amazing catches in the outfield. The Orioles were held to five combined runs in the four losses.

THE VACUUM CLEANER

The 1970 regular season was nearly identical to 1969 in Baltimore. The Orioles finished 108–54. Cuellar, Palmer, and McNally each won 20 or more games. The offense put up an AL-best 792 runs.

Brooks Robinson won the AL Gold Glove Award at third base every year from 1960 to 1975.

After once again rolling through the Twins in the ALCS, Baltimore met the Cincinnati Reds in the World Series. This time Baltimore finished the job, thanks in large part to Brooks Robinson.

One of the greatest fielders of all time, the Orioles' third baseman put on a show over five games against Cincinnati. His nickname was "the Human Vacuum Cleaner" for his ability to slurp up ground balls hit his way. Against the Reds, he made several highlight-reel stops. And when he wasn't flashing his stellar fielding, Robinson was crushing the ball at the plate. He hit .429 in the series with two home runs and six RBIs. He was named World Series MVP after the Orioles clinched a five-game victory with a 9–3 win.

FINDING THE FORMULA

Baltimore once again reached the World Series on the back of a 101-win season in 1971. Cuellar, Palmer, McNally, and fourth starter Pat Dobson each won at least 20 games. Once again the favorite, the Orioles jumped out to a 2–0 lead on the Pittsburgh Pirates. But the inspired play of Pirates right fielder Roberto Clemente carried Pittsburgh back. In Game 7, the future Hall of Famer hit a fourth-inning homer off Cuellar to break a scoreless tie. The shot propelled Pittsburgh to a 2–1 win and a series victory.

Despite winning only one of the three World Series, Baltimore's run from 1969 to 1971 was one of the best baseball had ever seen. And under Weaver, Baltimore continued to win throughout the 1970s. The Orioles never had a losing record in the decade. However, the AL also had several other great teams. Baltimore's two playoff appearances in 1973 and 1974 were stopped by the eventual World Series champion Oakland Athletics. Baltimore finished second in the AL East Division each of the next three years behind the Boston Red Sox and New York Yankees.

It took until 1979 for Baltimore to reach the World Series again. In a rematch with the Pirates, Baltimore raced out to a 3–1 lead. But the Orioles scored only two total runs the rest of the series. Pittsburgh came back to win in seven games.

Eddie Murray was named the AL Rookie of the Year in 1977 after hitting .283 with 27 home runs.

HERE COMES CAL

By 1981 the Orioles still had Weaver and Palmer, but the rest of the roster looked very different. Slugging first baseman Eddie Murray was a young offensive star. The pitching staff now had lefties Scott McGregor and Mike Flanagan.

That year a local product made his major league debut at shortstop. Cal Ripken Jr. had grown up in nearby Aberdeen, Maryland. His father, Cal Sr., was an Orioles coach. The younger Ripken made his first start for Baltimore in August 1981. A year later, he was the team's primary shortstop. After hitting 28 homers in 1982, Ripken won AL Rookie of the Year. A year after that, Ripken was the AL MVP. His play helped push the Orioles back to the World Series.

THE I-95 SERIES

Travel wasn't much of an issue for the Orioles and NL-champion Philadelphia Phillies for the 1983 World Series. The two cities sit just 100 miles (161 km) apart. When moving back and forth for the games, both teams went by bus on the freeway. That earned the games the nickname "the I-95 Series" for the interstate highway that connects Baltimore and Philadelphia.

Cal Ripken Jr. led the AL in hits, runs, and doubles during his MVP season in 1983.

Although the travel was easy, hitting was a problem for both teams' star players. Ripken hit just 3-for-18. Philadelphia's star slugger, third baseman Mike Schmidt, was 1-for-20. Even with those bad numbers, the series still had drama.

McGregor was cruising through seven innings of Game 1. Entering the top of the eighth inning, he had six strikeouts in a 1–1 tie. Before he could start the inning, a strange delay interrupted the game. President Ronald Reagan was in attendance. In between innings he was interviewed by the television broadcast crew. The interview went long, and the players had to wait it out. All the while, the Baltimore starter's arm was getting cold.

EARL SAYS GOODBYE

Cal Ripken Jr.'s rookie season of 1982 was also Earl Weaver's last during his first run as the Orioles' manager. Since taking over in 1968, Weaver had not posted a losing record in any season. He returned to manage the team for the final 105 games of the 1985 season and went 53–52. But the next year, the Orioles finished 73–89. Following the season, Weaver retired for good with 1,480 victories.

When the game finally resumed, Philadelphia outfielder Garry Maddox crushed McGregor's first pitch for a home run. The shot proved to be the difference in Baltimore's 2–1 loss.

That setback didn't seem to bother the Orioles for the rest of the series. Baltimore fell behind in each of the next three games. All three times the Orioles rallied to win.

Like Ripken, Murray struggled through the first four games. But in Game 5, the first baseman broke out of his slump. He hit his first home run in the top of the second inning for a 1–0 lead. Catcher Rick Dempsey, the series MVP, then made it 2–0 with a solo shot in the third. After Ripken walked to lead off the fourth inning, Murray socked another homer. McGregor, free from presidential interruptions,

The Orioles celebrate at Philadelphia's Veterans Stadium after winning the 1983 World Series in five games.

did the rest. He pitched a complete-game, five-hit shutout to seal the Orioles' first championship in 13 years.

THE OLD AND THE NEW

After being one of the most successful MLB teams for two decades, the Orioles took a steep fall for the rest of the 1980s. By 1988 several World Series stars were gone. Baltimore was one of the worst teams in baseball. That year the Orioles started 0–21, the worst season-opening losing streak in MLB history. Baltimore surprised the league a year later by bouncing back and competing for the AL East title. But for the most part, the Orioles were going nowhere in the standings.

Baltimore still found a way to change baseball forever. Starting in the 1950s, many baseball teams began playing in stadiums also built for football. Before that era, most ballparks were unique. But the shared stadiums lacked charm.

Oriole Park at Camden Yards cost $110 million to build in the early 1990s.

As the Orioles constructed their new ballpark in time for the 1992 season, they looked to the past. The result was a retro ballpark that became the envy of the league. Its full name was Oriole Park at Camden Yards. But fans quickly shortened it to just Camden Yards. The name came from the old train yard on which the park was built. Over the next three decades, many new MLB parks took inspiration from Camden Yards. Baltimore's new gem became known as "the Ballpark That Forever Changed Baseball."

PAPAL VISIT

On October 8, 1995, Pope John Paul II visited Camden in one of his seven trips to the United States in his time as pope. The park hosted the Holy Father's papal mass with an audience of 50,000 people. There were reportedly twice the number of reporters at this event as at Cal Ripken's record-breaking game.

IRON MAN

The Orioles opened their new home on April 6, 1992, with a shutout from veteran pitcher Rick Sutcliffe. Even though Baltimore won 89 games that year, it wasn't good enough to make the playoffs. Still, more than 3.5 million fans came through the doors at Camden Yards. And those who did knew they would see Baltimore's star shortstop in the lineup every day.

Cal Ripken Jr. had not missed a game for the Orioles since May 1982. By the end of the 1993 season, he was in sight of Lou Gehrig's record of 2,130 consecutive games. Ripken was on track to surpass the New York Yankees great early in 1995 if he could stay healthy.

At one point during Cal Ripken Jr.'s iron-man streak, he played 8,243 consecutive innings.

However, in August 1994 a wrench was thrown into Ripken's plans. MLB players voted to go on strike. The labor standoff stretched well into the spring of 1995. Many owners around the league began spring training with replacement players. The Orioles' owner, Peter Angelos, refused to do so. He was prepared for the Orioles to sit out the 1995 season if his starters did not come back.

If the Orioles didn't play, Ripken's streak would end. But in April, the players and owners finally worked out a deal. The season would start late and be shortened from 162 to 144

Mike Mussina won 19 games in 1996 to help the Orioles get back to the playoffs.

games. But the regular players, especially Ripken, would not miss any action.

When baseball did resume, many fans did not come back right away. Angry at rich players and even richer owners for taking baseball away, many stayed home as a protest. Those who did show up heckled both sides for being greedy.

As the summer wore on, more fans started to forgive. A big reason for this was the building interest in Ripken's streak. He had long been one of baseball's most humble and well-liked stars. Fans all over the country got behind the shortstop. Finally, on September 6, Ripken suited up in game number 2,131. A sellout crowd attended the game. Another huge audience watched the national cable broadcast at home.

END OF THE ROAD

Ripken was still the centerpiece of a slugging Baltimore lineup the next year. But he also had plenty of help. Center fielder Brady Anderson set a team record with 50 home runs. Six other Orioles, including Ripken, hit at least 20. That power, combined with the pitching of righty Mike Mussina, sent Baltimore back to the playoffs for the first time since its World Series win in 1983. However, another playoff run in 1997 was the last for an aging lineup. Every one of Baltimore's starting fielders in 1998 was at least 30. Ripken was 37.

As the team wound down a disappointing 79–83 season, Ripken finally decided it was time to take a break. Shortly before the start of a game against the Yankees on September 20, Ripken asked to sit out. After the first out of the game, Ripken received a long standing ovation from the fans inside Camden Yards. His teammates joined in, as did the Yankees' players. His streak had finally ended at 2,632 games.

MURRAY'S MOMENT

In 1996, on the one-year anniversary of Ripken breaking the consecutive game record, Eddie Murray hit his 500th home run. Once he did so, he became the third player in MLB history with at least 500 homers and 3,000 hits. He received an eight-minute ovation from fans after the historic blast.

FLIGHTLESS

As Ripken's career wound down, Angelos looked for new stars. The Orioles' farm system was no longer developing players as it had 30 years earlier. And Angelos was trying to keep pace with the high-spending Yankees and Boston Red Sox in the AL East. The aggressive owner tried several expensive moves. He signed former AL MVP Miguel Tejada to play shortstop in 2004. That same year, veteran catcher Javy López was brought in from the Atlanta Braves.

The next season, Baltimore traded for slugging right fielder Sammy Sosa. When Sosa arrived, he had 574 career home runs. But he hit only 14 in his one season with Baltimore.

While the Orioles searched everywhere for star players, the team struggled. At one point, fans protested outside Camden Yards, calling for Angelos to sell. From 1998 through 2011, Baltimore never finished higher than third in the AL East.

SHOWALTER'S SHOW

Late in the 2010 season, Angelos hired veteran manager Buck Showalter to run the team. That year the Orioles lost more than 90 games for the sixth straight year. However, they did have some young talent. Young catcher Matt Wieters had developed into one of the best at his position. Center fielder Adam Jones, just 25, had already been an All-Star.

After joining the team in 2008, Adam Jones was a five-time All-Star during his 11 seasons in Baltimore.

With additions like slugging first baseman Chris Davis, the Orioles' turnaround came quickly. In 2012 they improved to 93–69 and won the AL wild-card game over the Texas Rangers. Though the Yankees ended Baltimore's season in the AL Division Series (ALDS), things were finally looking up.

Two years later, the Orioles won their first division title since 1997. Jones, Davis, and veteran designated hitter Nelson Cruz each hit more than 25 home runs. Closer Zach Britton anchored a solid pitching staff. Baltimore finally made more playoff memories at Camden Yards with a sweep of the Detroit Tigers in the ALDS. The highlight came in Game 2, with a rally from 6–3 down in the bottom of the eighth inning. Pinch-hitter Delmon Young's three-run triple capped the comeback in a 7–6 win.

MARYLAND MELTDOWN

The Orioles' Game 3 victory over the Tigers in the 2014 ALDS was their last playoff win for years. Baltimore was swept by the Kansas City Royals in the ALCS. Two years later, Baltimore lost the AL wild-card game to the Toronto Blue Jays. The following season began a quick downfall.

Davis became a symbol for the team's struggles. In 2013 he set an Orioles single-season record with 53 home runs. But Davis also struck out a lot. In 2015 and 2016, he fanned more than 200 times each season. Angelos still awarded him a huge contract in January 2016. Even worse, when Davis wasn't hitting home runs, he struggled to hit at all. In 2017 Davis had just 98 base hits, 26 of which were home runs. He struck out 192 times and hit just .168.

As Davis struggled, so did the rest of the Orioles. Young stars like third baseman Manny Machado were traded away before Angelos had to give them raises. Two years after making the 2016 playoffs, Baltimore finished 47–115. It was the worst record in the franchise's 118-year history.

REBUILDING THE BIRDS

While the next few years weren't much better, the

Chris Davis hit 253 home runs in 10 years with the Orioles, but he also struck out 1,550 times.

Orioles did start collecting some promising young players. In 2021 center fielder Cedric Mullins became the first Oriole to hit 30 home runs and steal 30 bases in a season since the team moved to Baltimore. First baseman Ryan Mountcastle hit 33 homers at age 24.

The team also had a feel-good story in designated hitter Trey Mancini. In the spring of 2020, the budding star left the

Cedric Mullins's 30-home-run, 30-stolen-base season in 2021 was the first "30/30" season in franchise history since Ken Williams of the St. Louis Browns did it in 1922.

team to be treated for colon cancer. He missed the entire season while undergoing chemotherapy. After being declared cancer free in November 2020, he returned to the team in 2021 and hit 21 home runs. Mancini was named the AL Comeback Player of the Year after the season.

As 2022 dawned, the Orioles were still struggling but had several potential stars on the way. Catcher Adley Rutschman was considered one of the most promising players in the minor leagues. He made his big-league debut on May 21, 2022, and tripled in his third at-bat. Other top prospects were not far behind him. For a team that has always grown its best players at home, the new crop was a welcome sight for Baltimore fans.

TIMELINE

1901

The Orioles franchise begins as the Milwaukee Brewers.

1902

The team moves to St. Louis and becomes the Browns.

1922

Led by AL MVP George Sisler, who hits .420, the Browns have a rare winning season but fall just short of the AL title.

1944

The Browns make it to their first World Series as a franchise. They lose four games to two against their crosstown rival St. Louis Cardinals.

1953

After 52 years in St. Louis, the team moves to Baltimore and is renamed the Orioles.

1966

The Orioles sweep the defending World Series champion Los Angeles Dodgers. Three consecutive complete-game shutouts by Jim Palmer, Wally Bunker, and Dave McNally highlight Baltimore's first championship.

1969

Despite winning a team-record 109 games, the Orioles are upset in the World Series by the New York Mets.

1970

Led by third baseman Brooks Robinson's MVP performance, Baltimore wins the World Series 4–1 over the Cincinnati Reds.

1971

Baltimore reaches the World Series for a third consecutive season but loses 4–3 to the Pittsburgh Pirates.

1979

Baltimore reaches the World Series but again loses to the Pirates in seven games.

1983

Facing the Philadelphia Phillies in "the I-95 Series," Baltimore wins 4–1 to capture its third World Series title.

1992

Oriole Park at Camden Yards opens. The Orioles win their first home game at the new park on a complete-game shutout by Rick Sutcliffe.

1995

On September 6, Orioles shortstop Cal Ripken Jr. appears in his 2,131st consecutive game, breaking the existing "iron man" streak of Yankees legend Lou Gehrig.

1998

Ripken's streak of consecutive games played finally ends on September 20, after 2,632 games played.

2014

Under manager Buck Showalter, the Orioles defeat the Tigers 3–0 in the ALDS. It is the team's first playoff series win in 17 years.

2018

The Orioles finish 47–115, the franchise's worst winning percentage since the 1939 season.

TEAM FACTS

FRANCHISE HISTORY

Milwaukee Brewers (1901)
St. Louis Browns (1902–53)
Baltimore Orioles (1954–)

WORLD SERIES CHAMPIONSHIPS

1966, 1970, 1983

KEY PLAYERS

Brady Anderson (1988–2001)
Mark Belanger (1965–81)
Paul Blair (1964–76)
Rick Dempsey (1976–86)
Adam Jones (2008–18)
Jim Palmer (1965–84)
Boog Powell (1961–74)
Scott McGregor (1976–88)
Eddie Murray (1977–88, 1996)
Mike Mussina (1991–2000)
Cal Ripken Jr. (1981–2001)
Brian Roberts (2001–13)
Brooks Robinson (1955–77)
Frank Robinson (1966–71)
Urban Shocker (1918–24)
George Sisler (1915–27)

Bobby Wallace (1902–16)
Ken Williams (1918–27)

KEY MANAGERS

Hank Bauer (1964–1968)
Buck Showalter (2010–18)
Earl Weaver (1968–1982,
    1985–86)

HOME STADIUMS

Lloyd Street Grounds (1901)
Sportsman's Park (1902–53)
Memorial Stadium (1954–91)
Oriole Park at Camden Yards
    (1992–)

TEAM TRIVIA

BIG DEAL

The Orioles were involved in the largest trade in MLB history in 1954. Between November 17 and December 1, Baltimore sent seven players to the New York Yankees and received 10 in return. The Yankees got the better of the deal. New York received future Cy Young Award winner Bob Turley. The Yankees also got Don Larsen, who threw the first perfect game in World Series history two years later.

POWER PITCHER

Baltimore ace Dave McNally helped his own cause in Game 3 of the 1970 World Series. He became the first pitcher ever to hit a grand slam in a World Series game. It was actually the second grand slam hit by an Orioles pitcher that postseason. Mike Cuellar hit one in the ALCS against the Minnesota Twins.

SO LONG, EARL

Earl Weaver was ejected from 96 games in his career, fourth-most in MLB history through 2022. That includes two instances in which he was thrown out of each game in a doubleheader.

FAMILY AFFAIR

Cal Ripken Sr. was named the Orioles' full-time manager in 1987. That year his shortstop was Cal Ripken Jr., and his second baseman was his younger son, Billy. The team posted a 67–95 record with all three Ripkens on board. Cal Sr. was fired after starting the 1988 season 0–6.

GLOSSARY

ace

A team's best starting pitcher.

batting average

A player's number of hits divided by their number of at-bats.

closer

A pitcher who comes in at the end of the game to secure a win for his team.

farm system

In baseball, all the minor league teams that feed players to one major league team.

franchise

A sports organization, including the top-level team and all minor league affiliates.

minor league

A lower level of baseball in which players work on improving their skills before they reach the major leagues.

ovation

Long applause by an audience, usually done while standing

pinch-hitter

A person who bats in place of a teammate.

players strike

When players refuse to work due to a disagreement between them and their employers (teams) about things such as working conditions or wages.

shutout

A complete game in which a pitcher allows no runs.

MORE INFORMATION

BOOKS

Flynn, Brendan. *The MLB Encyclopedia*. Minneapolis, MN: Abdo Publishing, 2022.

Gitlin, Marty. *MLB*. Minneapolis, MN: Abdo Publishing, 2021.

Hewson, Anthony K. *GOATs of Baseball*. Minneapolis, MN: Abdo Publishing, 2022.

ONLINE RESOURCES

Booklinks
NONFICTION NETWORK
FREE! ONLINE NONFICTION RESOURCES

To learn more about the Baltimore Orioles, please visit **abdobooklinks.com** or scan this QR code. These links are routinely monitored and updated to provide the most current information available.

INDEX

ABOUT THE AUTHOR

Steph Giedd was previously a high school English teacher, but she is now a sports editor. Originally from southern Iowa, Steph now lives in Minneapolis, Minnesota, with her husband and pets.